Fragments of the Past:

Post-Traumatic Poetry

by samantha tamburello

To request permissions contact the author tamsamburello@gmail.com

Cover art by Sara Lauth, 2021

Published: New York, United States of America

author's note

i've had a remarkable talent the past decade of keeping so incredibly busy that i don't deal with my problems. during the covid-19 pandemic, it got quiet and i began to reflect on my life and a series of traumatic events that shaped me. with that came pain and soon, i began to heal. this book chronicles that journey and helped me so very much. i hope it can help you too.

the book is divided into 2 sections aligning with my experiences, section 1 "processing" and section 2 "healing..." which is shorter in length but of course, this chapter has not ended yet.

trigger warning: themes involving mental health, trauma, sexual assault and su*cide. please read with caution and be well.

1:
Processing

i told you i felt sad,
unable to express the magnitude.
you laughed at me.

i wrote poetry to express my feelings,
you told me to write happier things.
so i leave you with a book about pain.

if you should find yourself in a quarantine
i suggest you stockpile.
stockpile the numbers of those you love most
as you won't be seeing them for a while.

if you should find yourself in a quarantine
i implore you to wear a mask.
whenever you go out you'll tell people you're fine
even though you wonder why they ask.

if you should find yourself in a quarantine
i beg you to find a hobby.
a whimsical hobby to replace your jobby
with the money you won't be making.

if you should find yourself in a quarantine
learn a new recipe.
you'll eat and eat into the night
to fill the void of a nightmare with no ending in sight.

my memories are becoming
a jumbled twisted stew.
a distorted misty figure.
one memory triggers another
and they both taste fabricated
in their content —
perhaps it was a dream,
some weird case of deja vu.
sometimes a memory is
a feeling
that i can't pinpoint.
a lingering, looming air
of negativity in my chest
weighing me down.
faceless men and women
saying words that hold no water.
a winter chill on a summer day,
rainfall in my living room.
a nostalgic potluck
of wondering if i've already
been on this long journey before.

i thought i was a dreamer
but with each stride i learn
the grass is always greener.
i'm losing my sense of direction
my perception of reality,
missing the mark of my intention.
trying to assemble the collection
of puzzle pieces that don't attach.
direction and motivation seem to align
but one without the other is a warning sign.
winding down into a maze-
it amazes me how i can take 10 steps forward
in the wrong direction
with no assistance or detection.
i suppose i'm missing an intuition,
a sound in my heart to which i'd listen.
some kind of mind mentor to say "keep going"
but i continuously go on knowing
there's a dead end ahead
so each morning i wonder
why do i get out of bed?

i never imagined that everything
i thought was real would be fiction.
i never imagined that sunlight
would betray me the way it did-
masked behind storm clouds of grey
for an army of months.
if not even consistency then
what can i trust?

low self-esteem is
hoping to hear something that
will make me feel whole.

affable in all appearances,
visage clean and calm
but it doesn't show what's inside her
or what storm's about to come.
we all have something inside us,
something tainted in sin.
we try to push it far away
but sometimes it will win.
the monsters that live inside us
do not mean us any harm.
they are the army of the broken,
the grieving and the worn.
they live within all of us
and sometimes do us harm.
often they are so well-hidden
that ourselves are the enemy sworn.
be gentle to the sinners
hell is no place for us.
we're all trapped in the cycle
of pain and grief and abuse.

committing the "unalive"
the unknown deep dive.
taboo in nature but only to those
who find it so foreign and opposed.
some people think of the concept each day.
consider it a way,
perhaps an escape.
or avoid it as it very well may seem
that it's closer than they can control,
a hazardous thought they deem.
it loses its sense of wonder and whim
when it dances within
a thought you cannot erase
a dreary headspace
not at all in the plan
but then again
what is?

i guess these have become
the pandemic pages.
these walls have become
therapy-
forcing me to relive everything i let go of.
my therapist has become
torture-
making me discuss the things i suppressed
comfortably at rest on a shelf somewhere,
visible but not in reach.
every morning begins the cyclical suffering.
thought after thought after thought after thought.
i need someone
anyone
i need to go somewhere
it doesn't matter where
but i'm trapped
and all i can do is think.
the hobby that is killing me.

i wonder if your eyes
saw something different than mine,
not in people
or objects
but hue
and saturation
and maybe your ears heard music
in a different octave
and maybe your tongue tasted food
in a muted fashion.
i wonder if the reason you smiled so much
was because you were tired of crying
and i wonder if you were so kind
because your life wasn't.
i am here
picking up the pieces of your existence
and i wish i knew
what made your journey come to an end.

—good night sweet prince

pigs in a blanket
figs in a basket
childhood's taste
crashed in my mind
last night-
i couldn't smell
or see
or hear
because the taste
of nostalgia
wiped out my other senses.
i cried in mourning
of my innocence
and grieving the girl
with dreams bigger
than this decrepit life.
i cry for her knowing
the disappointment
she would feel
for knowing she would go through so much pain
and in the end, it would win.

that black and white photo
reminds me of you.
it reminds me of my world
when i was with you.
filling in the blanks,
imagining i saw things differently.
the excitement i imagined,
the color i longed for.
you were certainly colorful,
do not think otherwise.
however you were the crayon
i was afraid to pick up.
so in turn, you chose me.
missed opportunity.
lack of excitement.
disappointment.
moments of the past.

the soul-sucking leech that hangs onto me.
pointing out every possible danger
every flaw that i may have
everything that could go wrong
and putting fire under my feet
as if to tell me it's all terribly urgent.
crisis mode is always.
irregular breathing is promised.
the way i bite my inner cheek
until it bleeds is an added bonus.
it is a disease that worsens
crippling you, if untreated.
when treated, he is still there.
taunting you.
teasing you.
testing you-
in agility and strength.
telling you it was never him
but was within you all along.

—anxiety

engulfing the brain
drowning the lungs
plaguing the sane
the stories unsung.
the car that crushed him
the depression that rushed in
the cancer that took her
his breathing was labored.
i can't unsee the image of grey ears
misshapen head on the pillow
their unlived years
haunted me and still does.
i don't have survivors guilt
i just have this theory
that some people are more equipped
to exist fully and simply be here
when i just exist with dread in my head
and this feeling *still wondering*,
why get out of bed?

i want someone to listen
i want someone to care
not when i'm gone
but while i'm still here.
and yet i wonder
if the reader of these words
is only reading them
because i'm already gone.

i like to laugh,
i like to joke with people,
complete strangers,
to see them smile.
i think i'm so afraid of the space distancing
myself from new people
i'm so afraid they will not like me
a stranger— that i'm afraid won't like me
that i'm forced to start my standup act
to checkout cashiers and train conductors.
i wonder where the line is between funny
and terribly pained and emotionally exhausted.
i wonder if that's why the funny people
hurt so bad.

i see you as you were in my dreams.
you look so beautiful
your smile is contagious.
we talk about tv shows and music.
your hair freshly washed and nails manicured.
you go places and have opinions.

now you are just the shell of her.
we talk about the weather and deer.
you don't smile.
you don't look well kept.
you don't watch tv or listen to music.
you don't think much or have passions.

sometimes before bed i think of you,
hoping to go back to the place where she exists.
i miss her so much.
mom i miss you.

it's okay to be sad, my friend.
i am sad too.
perhaps we'll share in our misery
when we look up at the same moon.
you can even cry,
the moon would never know.
although i might feel it,
kindred sadness resides in the soul.

existing for the respite.
knowing my head will rise
above the high tide.
my feet will be regrounded
simultaneously my head will stop
spinning
the wheel of misfortune rests for
a breath
my lungs replenish.
the rush of air
the resuscitation
i'm brought back to life
i live
and thrive
only waiting for
the respite.

familial ties
and sickening lies.
the façade that they will stick by.
maliciousness drips
from sheepskin so white
draped over the nightmare
of evil in plain sight.
pillar of the community,
if that community were hell
bacon to a pig, the man could sell.
words come so fluid, so easy for he
who knows how to manipulate
groom and then flee.
family is nothing but a word to me
i'll chop our ties with scissors
then sleep like a baby.

biting the scars on my inner cheeks
a noticeable tremor when i attempt to speak.
my hands are shakey,
feet a little earthquakey.
rock bottom is miserable
but what feels even worse
is revisiting it once again
thinking i've been cursed.
healing is slow
never linear
you will often
furrow your brow when you realize,
"i've been here."

headphones that dangle at rest,
decorative ear ornaments at best.
my thoughts create music, not my genre
a loud monstrosity hidden in timbre.
after many minutes my thoughts decay
as i realize i still haven't pressed play.

—mind music

you were getting sicker
and i wished i could go
someplace else.

the depression got thicker
and i wished i could go
someplace else.

the nights grew lonelier
and i wished i could go
someplace else.

i didn't know where home was
and i wished i could go
someplace else.

now i am someplace else.
and i wish i could go
someplace else.

i'm realizing i cannot escape
from myself.

i'm not afraid of heights
i'm afraid of falling
i'm afraid of situations
that i cannot control.
i'm afraid of the unknown
and the great big unknown
where will i go
after i go?
i'm afraid of feeling
because i feel so deeply
and i'm afraid of time
because it moves so quickly.
i'm afraid of absolutely everything
that cannot be explained
and unfortunately for me,
the list grows.

i'm unsure how it turned out this way
such pain in our hearts,
sitting in joint isolation
37 miles away, i checked
but i still somehow can't answer your calls.
it brings me such pain to hear your voice
on the other line echoing on the walls
a little skip in your voice when i suggest
maybe i'll come over next weekend,
so we can sit in joint isolation
in separate rooms,
alone together.
as i scroll on my phone
and you experience your own distorted reality
in an empty room where you sit alone
and converse with dozens of people.
then we'll order pizza
which we won't eat together
and i'll pretend everything's fine
despite fate turning life as i knew it on its head.
sipping water from the same glass i used
when i was 8 years old
when my biggest fear was you dying
and now my biggest fear
is never getting you back.

healing seems to be an olympic sport. nobody told me talking about it would leave me sore. or that thinking about it would reveal scar tissue. nobody told me that processing would change the tint of the world and leave a funny taste in my mouth. nobody told me that healing hurts more than forgetting. at least forgetting was a paradise of ignorant bliss but this new place seems to have a lot of boxes to unpack.

i found my voice,
finally spoke.
you clasped a hand over my throat.
my voice was not the pitch you wanted
the words tainted, dark and haunted.
though i spoke out against him
your stance was clear, one of protection.
you defended the person who hurt me deeply
your intentions set against me, very clearly.
i do not regret finding my voice
but wasting it on you was my regretful choice.

my body is a hallucination
my senses are a manifestation
of my disillusioned reality.
i am a tree
deep rooted
deep seeds
deep-seated
worry.
much to give
nothing to take.

—the grieving tree

in my darkest times i often find
my darkest nightmares come alive.
a dark figure resembling hell;
and right out of my own mind she fell.
sporting her inner crimson fuel
across her rotting skin; so cruel.
so abrasive, so incredibly raw.
out of the dark lagoon she crawled.
out of my mind and right in my face
my own dark self i couldn't escape.

"optimism" she said in response to my unenthusiastic impending good news . i replied without even a thought, "i have none of it". why was this my response to potential good news? why am i never excited for myself? why does good news translate to "what could go wrong?" and why do i assume the worst when opportunity knocks? these questions may be in part due to the anxiety that i took years to address and rarely face. but also, it's simpler. i believe i was born optimistic. i was an excitable child. i always looked toward the positive and exciting things happening. i kept countdowns of every birthday, holiday and vacation. but now, within every birthday is fear, within every holiday is stale nostalgia and within every vacation is a countdown until it ends. perhaps this is what we call "growing up". perhaps maturity happens when our eyes begin to shift to the negatives. to keep us safe. and aware. and in control. but what good does it do? and why is it so difficult to revert to simpler times when you never meant to change?

—growing pains

i'm wrestling with what version of myself
i want the world to see.
i want to be seen as happy
but i don't want to be a pretender.
i want to be seen as effervescent
but i don't want to hide that i'm drowning.
i want my voice to be sing-songy
and carry across the room
the way it used to
but every note i utter is so very bland.
my voice carries about 3 feet away
and collapses.
people ask me how it's going
and i laugh and say "can't complain".
i'm laughing at a question
so impossible to answer
and i'm laughing at my answer
which so dramatically contradicts
my days, my nights, my weeks months and years.
i'm doing everything i can to stay afloat.
i wonder when i'll get the water out of my lungs.

nothing is fulfilling
the negativity is drilling
on my fragile brain
distorted, from once sane.
reaching for a handle,
more than i can handle.
looking for stability
a moment of tranquility
but the world's so dynamic,
it's turning me manic.
i'm just an average person
but the absolute worst version.
caught in the high tide,
life's a fucking ride.

i'm not who i want to be
but i'm who i need to be.
i didn't choose these trials.
tribulations trying my patience
trying my dry eyes
how many tears will we cry tonight?

i'm not who i always pictured.
an imagination as vivid as life itself
and yet i could never imagine myself here.

i am not the person who i want to be.
i am a person shaped by circumstances.
the bad kind.
i am irritable and anxious.
i am tired
of the days and years.

i'm not who i want to be
but if i picture myself with lower expectations
maybe i'll be half way there.

the internal dialogue, never-ending monologue within me. how sweet and magical that she is always with me, always commenting on something, an analysis to offer, and of course, always letting me down. the worrisome whisper that my voice seems to contrast. i grow older, paralleling my sadness of how much i want her to be silent. i do not identify with her voice nor do I value her words. she is each brick building up my walls, she is every fixed follicle, every unnecessary unit of manipulative measure. i want to be a fluid figure flowing through my days but she has me stuck in this staccato sort of nightmare. you cannot brainwash your own brain nor reverse it. you cannot flush the negativity down the drain. i embody her convoluted chaos with every lowering of my head and holding of my breath. she hides behind gritted teeth and tiptoes on eggshells. speak out. listen to your heart. don't hide who you are. this is what they say but they never dare ask if she is who i want to be seen. there is no confidence in the convoluted chaos, no hope nor optimism. she needs help far more than she'll lead you to believe. perhaps the journey lies in a destruction, a reconstruction, a rebirth and a great masking along the way. but as for the internal dialogue, that cannot go away.

i'm trudging uphill in the sand,
ankle and wrist weights secured.
the wind is blowing sand in my eyes
but i'm trudging still with such urgency
because that's what they say you have to do
but it's a fine line between carrying on
and taking care of yourself.
what they're asking me to do
is not what my body tells me.
as a sandstorm erupts around me
and my legs are ready to give out
a neon sign lights up
so as to remind me
that only the weak rest.

oh, so many things you ruined.
not with your hands
but by association.
by being near you,
with you,
coming out of your mouth.
i feel a little sick
when i hear a football game
and i feel queasy when i see sailboats.
you ruined so many things
and people
and places.
and i'm more mad at myself now
for not being able to enjoy them anymore.

my words are glued inside my head,
my body is glued inside my bed.
my lips are glued together whenever possible
so when i speak it is hardly even audible.
i wish to disappear into thin air
i'll still be here, but they'll never know where.

the name of the game
is self-sabotage,
the object is to hate myself
so incredibly much
i will destroy relationships,
sever ties with close friends,
isolate,
and hopefully disintegrate.

peering eyes and unintentional lies,
vindictive people falling from the sky.
a storm surrounds us coughing up gases,
we'll bolt our doors until it passes.
games of torture thrust upon you,
i'm wondering the day when it will be through.
locking my door, sleeping with the light on,
air filter on high until they're all gone.
i look up to you, you're all that i have
but sometimes it seems we've both gone mad.

—delusions by proxy

it's the shade being down,
collection of socks bedside
beside the empty water bottles.
it's the journal pages ripped
crumpled to the floor-
an attempt at fake positivity
writing poems about love
despite a self-hatred that runs deep
through my veins pumping like
gasoline, i'm on empty
but though my stomach cries out,
my body's last attempts,
i cannot find it within me.
it's my body and my mind
not seeming to align.
my body says 'save me'
my mind says 'what for'?

it seems like my life
is one long mathematical equation
that i'm unable to solve.
the variables are nonsensical,
nothing seems to add up.
no matter how much energy
i pour in,
writing
erasing
until my hands bleed
my efforts do nothing.
but i have learned
what not to do
and more importantly
my threshold,
which over the years
weens thinner.

a year, however hard it tries,
will always be time.
a moment so fixed
so finite by nature,
how can it bring variables
so unpredictable and raw?
how can it deviate from expectation
stirring up situations you could never imagine?
they say time heals all wounds,
but each year i tape up the wounds and wince,
so as long as years are a measure of time
i'll count on nothing to heal my wounds.

why does everything seem better in retrospect?

we have so much trauma in the past and yet it still
seems better than living in the present.

i imagined my life would be so much different than this. i imagined dumb nights on rooftops and glowing sunsets with first kisses and skateboarding through the middle of nowhere with a cigarette in my hand because i don't really care if i died, i was already doing everything i ever wanted to. i imagined new cities and new faces and relocating to new places where nobody knows me. being mysterious, walking aimlessly and dancing under the moonlight with champagne courage. i feel so stuck and so old.

you said i never think of you.
you couldn't be more wrong.
i think of you every time i'm able to smile
and every time i feel loved.
you deprived me of it for so very long,
i can't help but think of you every time.

disdain.
disgust.
distrust.
disassociation.
disappointment.
dis-appointed,
no longer in control
my emotions are on a roll
a cycle
a machine
pre-programmed
at the age of 7.
to repeat
disdain.
disgust.
distrust.
disassociation.
disappointment.

depressive state, you inspire me to write.
invading my mind day through the night,
a daydream of darkness, the grasp of an icy hand,
a summers day in a wintry cold land.

i couldn't compare you to a viper,
you are more hateful, dangerous and deep.
stark frost nips the robins of December,
similarly to your fangs dug into the meek.

to hate you is to count the ways-
i hate your mournful darkness and voices.
your quicksand grasp, disappearing me for days.
stealing my words, wisdom and choices.

you continue to cling your icy claws onto my heart
and i'll continue to look pretty as i silently fall apart.

—ode to depression

the survival instinct we all possess,
one i wonder if i've evolved past.
for the day came when i was asked
if i've ever had a near-death experience.
a complex question, to which i'd say
yes, i have it every day.

the painter-
the euphemism i use
to describe me
and my little white lies.
my happy disguise
so that no one asks why
or even bats an eye.
it is embarrassing to be
someone with a story.
to procure a level of shame
and believe you're to blame.
so i do not tell lies,
i paint pretty lines
over the cracks on the walls,
the chips, dents and all.
to tell a prettier story
of mystery and glory
and hope nobody can see
the way the wall used to be.

i am okay
the words we all say
as we melt off the earth
silently suffering since birth.

i am okay
maybe this is my day.
it's funny we all ask.
lying is our shared task.

i am okay
our fancy little way,
synonymous to say,
i am not okay.

i'm so sorry i'm not who you wanted me to be.
maybe i was too artsy where you wanted brains
or too emotional where you wanted logic.
maybe i cared too much when you cared none,
maybe i stuck around when you roamed off.
maybe i just love girls so fucking much
and you saw me tainted in sin.
i'm not sorry that i'm going to be me now,
i'm not sorry to not care.
i'm not sorry if you don't see me anymore,
i cared once but it's too much to bear.

i stopped feeling like me recently..

the ignorant butterflies floated away
and the concrete boots decided to stay.
a little of my sunshine made a great escape
when my brain decided to rewind the tape.
suppression tasted good for many years
but isolation has resurfaced my greatest fears.
the taste was bitter but hard to pinpoint
like a lingering pain from joint to joint.
then i couldn't get his fucking face out of my head,
stayed awake for hours tossing and turning in bed.
then the acceptance that an innocence was stolen
and soon, the memories came rolling and rolling.
i showered for hours to feel a little cleaner
curled my lip in protection, to feel a little meaner.
built up my walls slowly, brick by brick
then noticed an exhaustion, my stomach sick.
i want people to like me and i want them to care
but here i am in my brick house, blatantly unaware
if people are gathering or having any fun
i simply sit here mortaring bricks, one by one.
healing will rest in finding the strength
to bottle my sunshine, get my butterflies caged.
my brick house will keep me safe, nonetheless
a window here or there would probably be best.
i am who i am and i cannot change the past
but what i do going forward will forevermore last.

i've seen the worst in everyone,
and my hamartia seems to be
that everyone, absolutely everyone
doesn't care what happens to me.
i have a chip in my shoulder,
a monstrous ugly chip
i hate the way i hate
myself more than the destroyers...
the trouble with being so worn down
is the camel's back is broken
and the straws continue to pile
on the carcass of my youth.
they tell me i'm so strong
and so resilient
but i cry when voices raise at me
and i assume the worst in everyone
because i've only see the worst of everyone.
every fight i have with someone
leaves another hole in my heart.
i try to please everyone
and i want to be well-liked
because deep down i know
i cannot take much more.
i've seen the worst in everyone
and i'm still waiting for the best.

murky, gloomy retrospect
where the high is tide
and the moods are low.
where everyone is selfish
and i am selfless.
less than my self.
everyone's desires
are at my expense.
and my desires
do not matter.
don't flatter yourself
if you're sad
nobody can hear you
except those who appreciate the anecdote.
i am a circus clown
the main act is that i'm a human being
and being sad isn't an option.
they'll throw pies in my face,
and dunk me under water.
it's not abuse
because they don't want it to be.
i'll ride my unicycle and honk my nose
and juggle knives, hoping if one jabs me
maybe someone will double-take.
but make no mistake—
they won't.

someone you greatly miss,
losing an heirloom in some sort of abyss.
dining alone on a cold wintry night.
an unfamiliar place with no one in sight.
foggy glasses that don't unfog.
a stuffy nose that won't unclog.
a rising rollercoaster that won't climax
unpacked boxes in stacks and stacks.
laryngitis in a crisis
an airplane flying with no pilots.
a feast to eat but no appetite
a creepy crawlspace with no light.
i do not wish it on you, friend nor enemy
for an optimistic soul it is the greatest anomaly.

—ode to depression part 2

my worth seems to be
what others think of me
and my value seems to lie
in if loved ones stick by.
i suppose it makes sense,
a self-loathing so dense.

my sensitivity doubled as your license to hurt me.
whether my limit is less than an average person was
never relevant. my limit was crossed. over and over
and over. and for that i will pay the price the rest of
my life.

my unconscious self is who i wish to be—
consciously,
dreams of screams at people i hate
and finally matching the energy irate
the nature of people's disgust toward me
created distrust and disillusioned reality.

my unconscious self effortlessly curates
a symphony of words, no need to hesitate.
she speaks her mind with so much ease
she is spunky and sassy, a bit of a tease.
a gorgeous gallivanting gazelle, no aim.
not surviving but thriving is her leisurely game.

my unconscious self, in dreamland galore
walks with her eyes high above the floor.
a confident curator of colossal capability
always on the prowl with strength and agility.
she will now and forevermore be
the girl i go to in my dreams, only.
i'll fall asleep fast so that i can see
the girl i wish i could be consciously.

the apocalypse of emotion seems to be upon us
as the stigma closes, out comes the trauma.
sharing stories dark and untold,
against the grain of society, something so bold.
i want to believe with time things get better
but each year brings a new scandal, a newsletter
a movement of people begging to be seen
a circle of survivors, some old some teen.
the society that believes mental illness is weird
is the same society that creates trauma and fear
leaving crumbs of chaos and disastrous dust
being malicious and then demanding trust.
funny how theres a stigma against the mentally ill
when we're being traumatized against our will.

do not yell at me.
i don't want to regress to
a scared child again.

they ask me how i could believe in ghosts
and aliens and other supernatural phenomena.
they laugh and question it as if
the absurdity of what we can see
isn't any stranger or scarier
than what we cannot.

—supernatural society

when the light in you died
a piece of me went with you.
to be so vibrant and colorful
drawing attention everywhere you went
to drawing an attention so different now.
i just want to protect you and keep you safe
if only you could help someone
who doesn't want to be helped.
if only i could respark the light in you
and go back to the way things were.
let me know if she comes back.
i have so much i want to tell her.

-mom

life in mute, tasteless grey
the only difference is the number day.
i don't even hear what people say,
never amazing but maybe okay.

odorless flowers, only the stem
only a rock never a gem.
the glass isn't half, only empty.
it's like a fever without the antibody.

the worst of everything but where's the best
they say to enjoy life and fuck the rest
but what if the rest is deliberately blocking the way
a great day for me is one that's okay.

there is a great hole within me
full of regrets and disappointment,
it swirls from my head to my heart
and down to my feet.
i can't walk,
i'm stuck
in this feeling
the great deep hole
of 'what ifs'.
it settles in my stomach
and knocks the wind out of me.
the wind creates a great hurricane
of horrendous memories gusting around
and falsified scenarios i create
about what could have been.
the post-traumatic tornado
rests for absolutely nothing
and tornado warnings don't exist
in this dreadful place.

dear heart,

i am terribly sorry to disclose
that grief will drown you head to toes.
that you will try to hide who you are
for people would kill you, near or far.
who you love will lose you friends,
loved ones will disapprove to no end.
you'll tape up mirrors to ignore
the person inside, lonely and poor.
you'll give up hope because you'll believe
nobody could love you and never leave.
you'll hide your identity even from yourself
destroying your physical and mental health.
I'm sorry heart, the journey will suck
but if you hold on tight it might be enough.

we're all just bubbling over
suppressing our emotions
to go with the flow and
impress other people
who are bubbling over
suppressing their emotions.
we're trying to piece together
the jumbled puzzle of the past
and if only we knew the missing piece-
the empty spot that we'll never heal from
lies in shared experiences,
the human need to fill the void
with other human connection.
to share in the misery, the pain
but instead
we bubble over
suppressing our emotions
to go with the flow
and impress other people...

dangling lights in my bedroom window.
this is about how festive i'll get.
i've said it once,
i'll say it again,
the seasonal affect is in full swing,
and i care not about one damn thing.
the snow is cold,
the plants are dead,
the only comfort is in bed.
everyone is a pretend christian for a minute,
making me feel inferior for 'sinning'.
the music plays,
slow and old.
nostalgia bowls me over
brash and bold.
i give out my presents,
as i hold back tears,
realizing all of my tangible fears.
nothing is what it was, things are changing.
my friends are moving away, i'm aging.
i had millions of dreams, which faded away
for now i just live day by day.

—merry christmas

you said you'll be a hawk in your next life,
gliding high above the treetops
but in the end, you were one in this life, too.
you were always the hawk, and i the mouse.
your precious prey to toy with all day.
you shaped me into a pathetic people-pleasing dud.
you skinned my confidence with your talons
and left behind a feathery fixation on my flaws.

it swells up in my chest
it's like a distant ringing
growing in volume.
and the oxygen saturation drops,
gravity holts for a moment,
and then i'm suspended there
with nothing to grasp.

low self-esteem,
the voice in my ear
telling me i deserve nothing here.
telling me i'm taking up too much space.
telling me to paint makeup on my face.
low self-esteem disguised as my voice,
making me think self-hatred is a choice.
burning me with guilt for being content,
burning me with guilt for trying to vent.
low self-esteem disguised as my voice…
i'm starting to recognize the verbiage of this noise
it was never me at all, i would never be this irate.
it wasn't me at all, it is only you i hate.

conditioned pessimism,
you ask me why i'm sad
but you never gave me a reason
to expect anything greater
than disappointment
and mountains of uncertain terrain.
i am conditioned like a machine
to prepare for what's to come
and when nothing ever does
the panic attacks set in and i feel like i'm drowning
on what ifs and when wills.
my sixth sense is my defense mechanism
to be sad and perhaps pleasantly surprised
when everything doesn't fall entirely apart.

with air in my lungs,
food on my plate,
water in my body,
blood in my veins
why do i feel like i won't make it?
maybe if i had nothing at all
i'd have a little more life in me.

—irony

time is the great eraser
a secret elixir, they say it'll fix her.
with each year that passed
she was forgetting quite fast.
each new chapter had brought
something exciting her attention had caught.
until it grew quiet and things became stable
and time turned back and she was unable
to withstand the memories playing on repeat
on the cinema screen, she's trapped in the seat.
to reach out for help is to try to explain
the plot of the movie to a mind too sane
to comprehend the jumbled nonsense and twists.
so she wells up with tears and clenches her fists.
perhaps this will all be over soon
and a new movie will start on a new moon.

in an empty room
an empty room inside me
words ricochet off the walls
and hit me, boomerang away
and back again to the same wound.
reverberating memories i want to forget.
voices i hate replace my own voice in my head,
as i whisper to myself repeatedly that i want to die,
unsure if they are words that i say or ones i mean.
i am desensitized to suicide,
the intrusive thought in my mind that replays,
the only song on the playlist on shuffle.
shuffling through my mind like eggs in a box,
bound to crack at any approaching shake.
as i walk to the train and whisper
that i'm going to kill myself,
i laugh it off knowing that i won't
but stare off into space as the train pulls away,
the unlocking brakes screeching against the tracks,
i try to drown out my thoughts
with the sounds of the city,
wondering where the line is
between a thought and an action.

i wish you knew me way back when
i laughed until i cried now and then.
the sky was bluer and it hardly rained
blue raspberry lips and matching shirt stains.
my list of friends went on and on
as for plans, i had a ton.
both events and life plans were in the book
i'm sure you probably would've mistook
that girl for some other one.
for surely i am not that fun.
i'd like to get back to her
but if it's possible — i'm unsure.

if each strand of my hair was another worry

then rapunzel i'd be

brushing my anxiety

trying to get it in order only to see

after i've finished it's still knotty

and detangler is the pills that i pop to no avail

the conditioner is my therapist whom i always fail.

i go to the hairdresser pleading with tears

to which she'll confirm the worst of my fears.

my hair ruins my life, this is true

but cutting your hair doesn't change you.

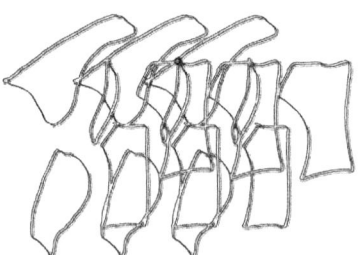

a world where
your living nightmare
is a show for all to see:
this spectacle of a genetic anomaly.
a chemical imbalance swooped in
and now they all stare, perhaps a slight grin
as if you've showered in sin
and now you drip scenes of the show
anyone can go,
admission is free to stop, to stare.
you're completely unaware,
a world where
nothing is fair.

dozens of miles away from the place i spent my
summers
climbing trees and becoming a woman
at the age of 7.
the river flowing behind the house
is the same river flowing past my apartment.
when i look at the water i see a scared child's
reflection staring back at me
wondering if things will get better.
they will,
but i can't help you yet.

i was set up for failure
in god's home as a young girl
when it was normalized to go
in a closed room with a grown man
to confess to him my wrongdoings.
they told me i should've known better
than to go in a closed bedroom
with a grown man
but how could i have known?

—toxic traditions

a symphony of suspense
a constant tick tock in my ear
prestissimo, synchronizing my heart
beating out of my chest.
i cannot breathe, only hyperventilate.
crescendo, tick tock tick tock,
the more aware i am the worse it gets
tick tock tick tock
i'm searching for an escape
a side door to run out of,
but it seems the door i need to exit
is the one within my mind.
exit stage left—
i can keep running out of the room
but the tick tock clock keeps ticking, fortissimo,
and my body thinks it's in a race.
it cannot rest until my mind can too.

— panic attack

2:

Healing...

there is great unity in sharing our stories.
though such pain comes from reflection,
what then comes is the triumph of humanity;
to share in our healing process
and what better balm
than that of human connection?

my biggest fear is also
the only thing that keeps me going.
the thing i detest the greatest
is my motivation and strength.
the looming grey cloud
is what i wince and walk toward.
my cement-filled sneakers
keep trudging down
the untraveled road
and my wandering eye
keeps on wandering.
and wondering.
my biggest fear
is quite wonderful.

-uncertainty

my joy was stolen
this is a simple fact.
if i keep forward rolling
i'm bound to get it back.
if i just sit in sorrow where i am,
i'll never feel like me again.

there's been a shift in the universe,
a shift in the stars
though the leaves are changing colors,
i know sunshine isn't far.
though the temperature drops low
my mood is rising high,
my body is moving with the flow
i feel this ethereal high.
i've been in a neutral gear shift
just barely coasting through my days
but with this sudden energy shift
i'm coping in unexpected ways.
i'm donating my smiles to those who need them so
and giving compliments to strangers and saying hello.
universe, i thank you for whatever this may be
energy shift, seasonal lift or something inside of me.

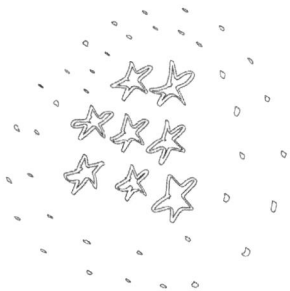

picking up the pieces of my life,
no i am not broken
i've been fragmented by strife.
the journey forward will be to collect
to reflect, and select
each piece to reassemble
a journey all mental.
i have nothing to lose
so each day i choose
another piece of my puzzle
the daily bustle
piece after piece
until the day when
i feel like myself once again.

a road leading to seemingly nothing at all,
red rocks ornamenting the periphery,
i look out as far as i can see and swear
i see hope glimmering in the distance.
the road signs urge me to proceed with caution
this is all so new and i am too young to know
what love is.
i am not in love with her,
i am discovering an overwhelming love for myself.
i am realizing for the first time,
i am allowing myself to feel
and love
and follow this road
with blind optimism.

—roadtrip

the grass is always greener
because that's how they paint it.
we are envious jealous creatures
because they'll flaunt the only thing they have.
i'm understanding now how
the people whom we assume have the least
have the most life fulfillment,
smiles to spare
and don't feel the need to paint their grass.

fragments of the past

i'm realizing how incredibly lucky i am
to be alive
sitting on this train
going to my job
to soon return home
to my stable life.
how lucky i am to write these poems
from my iphone
with clair de lune playing in my headphones,
as i type in my notepad about strife
and trauma
and all of the bad things
that are all far over now.
as the sun begins to peak
over the tall buildings
and the crisp air
settles and warms
and welcomes a new day-
i'm realizing how incredibly lucky i am
that i am me.

one thing about me that you should know
is i'm not a regular girl, i'm a superhero.
i'm constantly thinking, analyzing around me
with incredible density, focus and complexity.
when i'm sad, i don't cry, i soak
in emotions and an invisibility cloak.
i'll disappear into thin air
nobody will see me anywhere.
when i'm happy, i take off for flight
i glow like a lightbulb yellow and bright.
when i'm afraid i think quick, act rationally
do whatever i need to bring everyone to safety.
i'm always prepared, come what may,
for my superpower, anxiety, to save the day.

like a gust of wind
you swooped in to let me know
i am not alone.

i'm letting myself change
like the ocean's tides
like the moon's phases
like the solstice and the equinox
like the days, months and years.
i can't feel guilty moving in the direction
that life pulls me in.
i can only succumb to the pull
and control the things i can.
i am invigorated
by the fluidity of life.

though i have tried,
sat in this room all night,
i simply cannot make sense
out of nonsense.
the moonlight peeking
through my blinds,
giving me zebra stripes,
delivers me a soft reminder
that it's time for bed,
i can try again tomorrow
but i still will be unable
to make sense
out of nonsense.

perhaps i just need
a shift of perspective.
perhaps it is raining
because the heat was too draining.
perhaps it's dark
because the sun needs her rest.
and perhaps i hurt
so that when i feel better,
i'll fly.

healing is contradiction.
it is faking everything you need to become.
it is reading a book
wanting to skip chapters
and not.
it is bitter in taste
but sweet in composition.
it is writing poetry
through hysterical tears
knowing each painstaking moment
is making an easier tomorrow.
it is making amends,
it is forgiving myself
for forgiving the people who hurt me
for forgiving the people who hurt them
who are forgiving the people who hurt them.
if my journey is anything at all,
it is mine.
it is regaining control.
it is closing the book
and writing a new one.

i feel myself come back
in the petrichor morning
following the rain of night.
the dark, cold place
will end with peace.
i will inhale the day
and exhale the night.

—onward

the undertow
will let me know
when it's time to slow,
refresh my soul.
the low tide is why
i even try
and when it's high
i'll standby.
the fluidity of life
does not rest,
so i'll do my best,
on all life's tests.
move with the flow
never against the grain
a single grain of sand
with great power to withstand
the bad so i can enjoy the grand.

i'm not who you thought.
the perfect victim is mute
but i found my voice.

—in this haiku the mermaid gets her voice back

i let this depression be a lesson
as to my strength, resilience
and lack of suppression.

i know i'm not broken.
there was a time when happiness came
from the same things i do now.
a time when the chemical reactions in my brain
kept me, what they call 'sane.'
i am me, i always have been.
shaped by circumstance
and chemical reactions.
isn't that what we are?
circumstances and chemicals?

'good things come in small packages'
holds more significance in age.
i see how the serotonin releases
in smaller doses
and happiness comes
in due time.
rainbows are pretty,
pretty translucent
and winter is nice
from inside your window.
i'll take what i can get
and make what i can't take.

the marching band of my mind-
each instrument is uniquely its own
in impulsivity
in panic and worry.
the chaos of the music swells
around me
within me
i am not the conductor,
i hold no power to stop it
but maybe
i can request a song.

c'était une épreuve du cœur
quand je vous ai entendu parler
pour la première fois.
on n'a pas de relation platonique
avec un ange.

you cannot take
what you don't put out
so put forth
your happiest hugs
your sincerest smiles
and your wisest words
so the universe can return to you
optimism with a pretty bow on top.

—recycled positivity

the problem
is i'm trying to get through the week
trying to get through the months
and getting through the years.
i'm getting through my life
with the purpose of rest
when i could be resting
all along the way.

we're going to get through this
in small doses.
we're going to come out the other side
with whom we're closest.

i'm not happy today
but tomorrow
i'll be okay.
like a sponge
i'll soak up the sadness
and expel it all in my sleep.
come morning i'll absorb
the morning light,
feel it within me
and go on
bubbly and warm
only releasing my light
to those who could use some.

i'm a quilter-
quilting together my memories
into a beautiful piece of warm happiness
for i know my past has too much good to ignore.
i will patch on climbing trees
and building sandcastles with my brother
next to discovering a great love for classical music
and singing show tunes and arias in my bedroom.
i will zig zag stitch the love i had for my first cat,
whom held my hand through the difficult times
as i held her paw for her final breaths on this earth.
my quilt will be a work in progress,
i will actively seek more patchwork
and i will drape the quilt over me as a reminder
that the bad does not outweigh the good.

i'm longing for a time
that will never come.
the only time
is right now
and all i can do
is dance in the rain.

speaking out
seemed to be
the forbidden fruit.
i must admit
sinking my teeth in,
letting the juices drip down my chin
is sweeter than i thought it would be.
he who forbid it
shouldn't have commit it.
life is sweeter now,
i think i'll have another.

—forbidden fruit

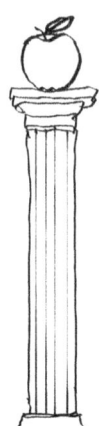

i'm done carrying heavy bags
under my eyes
losing sleep
over other people's actions.
i'm setting fire to the baggage,
dancing on the ashes.
scooping the charred remains
into my charcoal kit,
to later make art
because as you now know,
making art from shit
is my specialty.

sometimes you must ignite the wick,
set your world aglow,
become immersed in the new plan,
the logic that you once needed
but are nonetheless glad you now possess.
live freely with eyes to the future.
protected, safe, and an awareness
that what has happened has bettered you
but what's to come will enrich you.

—enlightenment

as we spin endlessly on this floating rock
having wars and dying of illness
finding purpose in the purposeless
i find that my panic is justified.
my body reacts to absurdity
and my mind is just painfully aware.

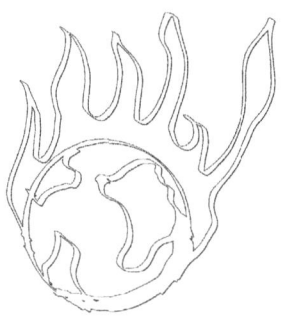

i've always fallen in love with people
who showed any single sign
that they understood me.
i'm learning now: i'm not an anomaly.
i'm a human being with strong mechanisms
of defense and self-preservation.
this realization is the self-love i've been missing.

with these fragments of the past
i will piece together a new beginning,
recycling my life into meaning
and painting a prettier picture
now that i hold the brush.

—fragments of the past

4000 days or so
i kept my mouth sewn.
i developed shame
when it should have been you.
too bad it took 6000 days or so
for the seams in my lips to burst.
i will [un]gladly tell anyone who asks
about the demon lingering under the mask.

—me too

what people see
when they look at me
is not at all what i want to be.
i am not cyclical anxiety,
thoughts about worry.
i am not someone in a hurry
to get home, where i'll go to bed.
there's a lot more inside my head.
i am made of flowers and poetry
and a little bit of magic and fantasy.
i am my dreams and my passions,
pastel colors are more my fashion
than the darkness often thrust upon me.
so the next time you look at me;
remember my situation
is not my destination,
it's just a stop
before my station.
i'll continue with a deep infatuation
for the flowers and magic
and fantastical sensation.

age 20 i thought i could hide it
for a lifetime more
but i made it about a week
before i fell to my knees
asking god why i had feelings
if it were wrong to have them.
i begged him to make me
whoever i'm meant to be.
i will gladly be straight
if that were his intention.
in another week's time
i flirted with a woman for the first time,
felt butterflies take flight within me
fluttering and dancing in escapade.
i never again was guilt-ridden,
never again concealed the person i am.
if i weren't meant to be this way
why would god say it's okay?
perhaps your god is just different than mine
and that is just perfectly fine
to have my own divine.

—my own divine

if you need someone,
i will hold your hand.
i will listen not to reply
but to understand.
i will guide you through
the chaos of your mind
and maybe on our journey
peace is what you'll find.

i thought life was purposeless
and i was right.
there is no purpose
other than to create purpose.
to plant seeds at the close of day
to have something to tend to tomorrow.
to have something pretty to look at later.

somewhere ashore this sea of orange cylinders
i'll find my head again, screw it back on
and commence where i left off.
for now, i'll keep wading
and waiting
and thanking poseidon
that my head's above water.

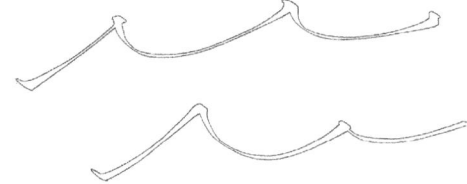

i was a broken stained glass window
split where the light shone the brightest.
most people have seen the crack
but you saw the art.
you traced your fingers along the glass
unafraid of being hurt,
in efforts to piece together the story.
there wasn't much of a story
until you came along to write it.
i gave you glue to fix the cracks
but you did not want it.
you found beauty in my glassy flaws-
my imperfections.
so instead, i offered you a paintbrush
to help rewrite the story.
you tilted the orientation
and changed it all completely.
there was no need for a brush
or a single drop of glue.
nothing was broken,
you taught me that.
what i saw in my own reflected glass
is you were there with me all along.

i opened the door
and there you weren't.
not everyone stays
and not everyone will see
the wonderful things i'll be.

there is nothing quite like
those brief moments
where you look in the mirror
and smile organically.
content with what you see,
even in shortcomings.
glossing over the laugh lines
put there by pretty quilt patches
and all the things that somehow
got you here, relatively unscathed.
thankful to your eyes for showing you
your strength and your ears
for hearing your little nose laugh,
not quite laughing but happily remarking
that you're here
and it's a beautiful thing
to just be here.

when the storm winds start
if all you can do is wait,
then wait. it will end.

—sometimes life is just waiting

National Suicide Prevention Hotline: 800-273-8255

Printed in Great Britain
by Amazon